leave the light on.

Emily Weaver

Cover design and illustrations by Emily Weaver

leave the light on.

Emily Weaver

Preface by the author

Everything that I write is simply a baseline for all of the ways you want to interpret them. Take my words as your guideline and then apply your own emotions, experiences and memories to make it your own. You won't relate to everything now, you might never relate to some, but hopefully there is at least something for everyone.

Always remember to look after yourself and prioritise taking care of yourself above others.

To the people drowning in darkness, find your own way to turn the light on

To find the light, you have to face the dark.

In reflection of life

Sometimes you don't really know who you are
- And that's perfectly okay

I don't know who I am,
Not in the slightest.

I don't know what my favourite song is.
I don't know who would pick up if I called.
I don't know why I like to watch the sun rise.
I don't know why watching movies makes me bored.
I have no clue who I am destined to be.
I struggle to pick just one favourite book.
I don't think labelling my sexuality will set me free.
I can't figure out how I want to look.
I can't remember what I did when I was nine.
I don't know why all of my friends leave.
I can't tell you why I always say I am fine.
I struggle to pinpoint what I believe.
I don't know why I am so curious.
I don't know why I always panic.
I can't tell you why your opinions make me furious.
I can't explain why my brain is so frantic.
I don't know who I used to be.
I don't know who I am now.
I don't know what the future holds.
I don't know what it means to be me.

The only thing that I can tell you for sure
Is that my favourite colour is purple,
And nothing more.

Sometimes you get your heart broken

- ***Sometimes you have to let your soul sparkle***

My heart is not broken,
Because I have never let anybody come close enough
To even peer into the vast chasm of where my heart resides.
No fingertips have wandered over the intrinsic details,
The intertwined threads of could have, would have and should have.
I have never felt the crushing weight
Of feeling a hammer collide with the centre of my personal globe.
I have yet to watch as the pieces settle into their new homes,
Detached and unwilling to reunite.

My heart is not broken.
How could it be when it does not ache for love?
It does not yearn for the embrace of its own kind
Or even consider its age-old fate.
It does not wish for another companion,
For someone to rip it from its safety
And let it crumble in the overbearing image of another place holder.

My heart is not broken,
But my soul is.

My soul is broken.
Because time and time again I search for answers where none can be found.
I wait for resolutions to disrupted pathways and uprooted notions,
The wavering ghosts of others haunt the depths of my insides.
The light within me flickers with understanding
As yet another person works the graveyard shift,
Bounding to end up alongside all of the others who passed through before.

My soul is broken.
How else could I describe the irreversible damage to the core of my strength?
The words that seep into pages and echo the experiences I have trudged through.
No other explanation for the turmoil which plagues my brain
And the light that refracts a hundred times when happiness sparks .

It is not split into a thousand pieces.
It is not shattered like a mirror overwhelmed by its significance.
It has escaped from its resting place where it enveloped my heart
And it wanders the lonely halls of my mind and body,
Searching for a place to call home,
Wondering what broke the line between coping and letting go.

My heart is not broken.
But my soul has become a kaleidoscope,
Waiting for its opportunity to break free and shine.

Sometimes you tear the page out

- ***Sometimes mistakes add character***

I map out my life like the plot of the next bestselling novel,
Adding chapters knowing that someday it will reach its conclusion.

Studying the individual characters and their personalities,
Weaving in the details which define one from another.
Each character, whether supporting or standing in the spotlight,
Is contemplated with calculated precision to affirm their position.
No character is forgotten, no memory is stuck to the page.
Chapters do not continue without the recognition of each existence
Which remains in the dried ink of the character's name.
Every soul which has lingered in the forefront of the novel's main plot
Will be honoured by the pages that they rest upon.
Not to be forgotten, but to be memorialised.

The world which is built upon in the imagination of one's mind
Exists in a way that is intrinsically unique to their perception.
A decision between whether the sun setting signifies
A letting go of the day which has just passed or
A welcoming of the day that is yet to begin.
Choosing whether to stop and smell the flowers as they pass by
Or forgetting to notice the true beauty of the world that they have designed.
The creation is always subjective to the thoughts of its creator.
The setting of a novel is crucial for some,
And for others simply a waste of time.

With background and history set into stone,
Each day begins with a fresh page of opportunity.
Will it be written in the pristine print of plain-sailing perfection?
Will it be smudged before the sand runs out of the upturned timer?
Will teardrops fall onto the half-written promises of the day ahead?
Will a jagged edge be all that remains to signify that hours have passed?

A journey can only be created from its obstacles.
A pathway can only be defined by its structure.
When they unite it toes the border between destruction and duty.

A story can only be told when it is finished;
This story can only be finished when it is told.

Sometimes you float in your own bubble

- ***Sometimes it is okay to pop it***

I like to think that between the hours of 11 and 3,
The world and I simply coexist.
I remain in a bubble of protection,
Whilst the world sings its sorrows outside.
I ground myself, breathing slow and deep,
And the world watches me through the windows.

I do not exist within the world in those moments,
I exist alongside it.
Turning on my own axis of despair and bewilderment,
Contemplating the means of joy and pleasure.

Sometimes you watch the time tick away

- ***Sometimes you have to stop and smell the flowers***

Because I find myself alone so often,
I have realised that the world around me softens,
The noises become dull and low,
As my thoughts bounce to and fro.

The beat of my heart pierces
Through the silence like a drum.
The wind echoes between crevices,
Whispering about storms that are yet to come.

I notice the tick of the clock
As it passes through the hours,
And sometimes I reckon I can hear
The drop of petals from the stem of flowers.

But deep in my soul
I know that I would rather
Hear the shushed laughter
Than the silence that feels so cold.

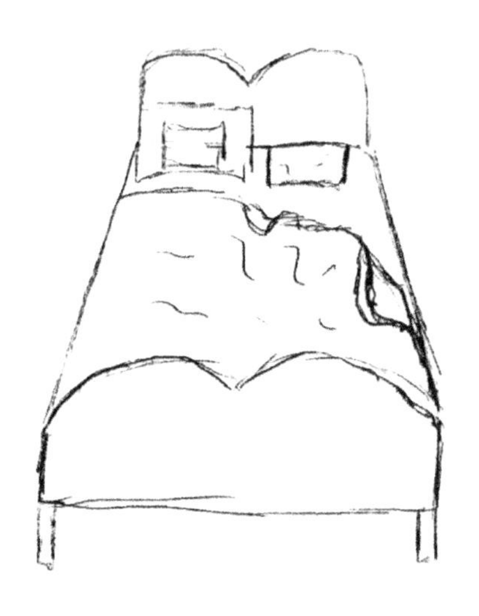

Sometimes you need to lay in bed all day

- ***Sometimes you need to force yourself out of it***

Lately nothing feels the way it once did.

I stay up until 2am just to avoid waking up
And having to face a new day.
And when I do sleep,
I sleep every one of my worries away
Because it is the only time I am truly at peace.
I struggle to read more than a few pages of a book,
Giving up halfway through words
Because my mind had already given up.
I get bored at what were my favourite shows,
Zoning out as the scenes switch,
Characters blurring before my eyes.
I lose track of time.
Seconds, minutes and hours ticking away,
Speeding up at the height of the day
And dragging out as the day comes to a close.
I can still feel the outline of who I used to be.
The hushed whispers of my soul,
Stuffed into the broken bones of my body,
Who are exhausted from the inside and out.

And nothing feels the way that it should.

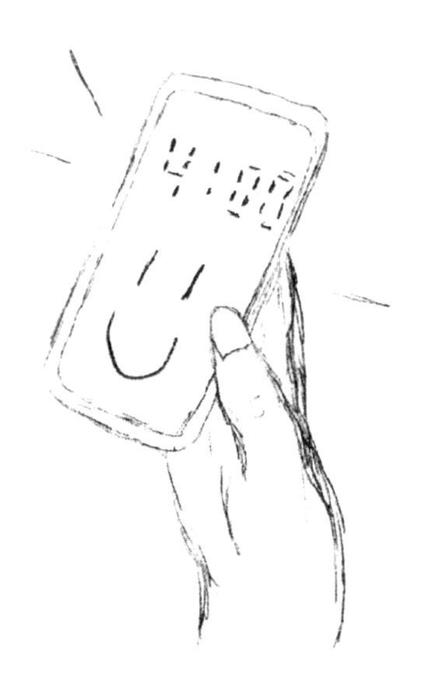

Sometimes you have to stay up until 4am in self-pity
- ***Sometimes you have to sleep and be thankful***

I stay up until 4am
Reading stories about love I'll never have,
Diving into worlds I'll never reach,
Grasping for friends that will never come.

I find myself entangled
In worlds far from mine,
Of concealed kisses
And true loves,
Of golden promises
And tender touch.

My eyes scan over every word,
Devour every single detail
And my mind questions,
My heart is racing in competition.

I do not sleep,
In the hope that the bubble
Of this fairytale reality
Will hold me,
Until it becomes mine.

Sometimes you feel like you can't breathe

- ***Sometimes breathing is all you can do***

When life gets tough I've learnt to escape.
I search for the space in the world
That I know let's the wind hit my face
And the sun brush my skin
And somehow just that tells me that I'll be okay.
It doesn't last long and
As soon as the sun fades I will too,
But that does not mean that it isn't worth it.
That those few seconds that
I stand with my eyes closed
And my thoughts far away from
The usual catastrophe of my mind,
Don't stand for every and any
Hope that I have for the future.
Because whilst I can, whilst I can breathe,
I have to remind myself that
I am still standing here.
The sun is still beaming and
The world is still breathing
And I get to stand at that one place in the world
And just take it all in for a second.
Let my worries become the earth's.
Let my future become my destiny.
Breathe just a little easier,
And see just a little clearer.
Escape.

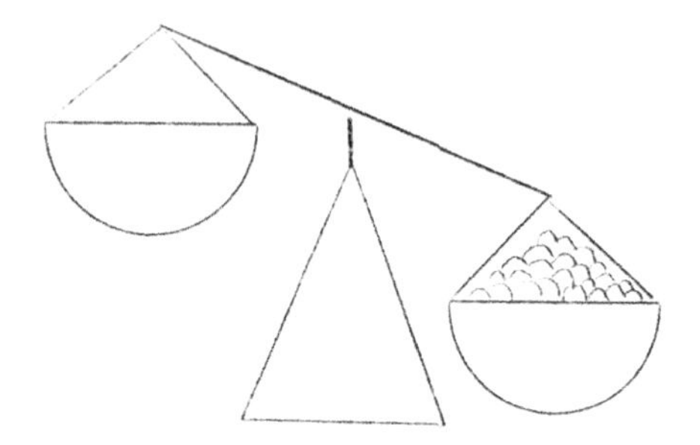

Sometimes you can let the scales tip
- ***This time you need to balance it out***

We live in a selfish world
And sometimes I struggle to understand it.

I fall victim to the novelties of life.
I take in the sickly sweet promises
And I endorse the media that boasts of perfect times.
I find it hard to grapple with reality,
To accept the systems that seem to have no beginning or end
Or to know why fate chooses certain people
To be society's shining stars.

Why am I so drawn in by the day to day life
Of an ordinary person living their dream?
Why does it make me wallow in self pity
And make my insides feel hollow and empty?

I hear whispers of the latest breaking news.
Whilst people suffer in silence -
Seeking shelter from the cold,
Bracing the rough icy sea,
Standing up for rights that should not have to be protested,
- Fighting for a chance to be free.

Why do we pay so much attention
To the fleeting nature of tomorrow's news?
Why do we seem to forget what is happening?
That we are the only ones able to spark the fuse,

To ignite the chance to change this world,
To change our greed and plant a fresh seed
Of promise, opportunity, hope,
A chance to finally succeed.

We live in a selfish world
Because we only ever think of ourselves,
Instead of taking a step back
To focus on,

A world worth fighting for.

Sometimes you shut the curtains on the world

- ***Sometimes you have to face it***

Why is the world so cruel?
It picks up the sunshine
And drowns it in the dark.
It takes the beams of light
And closes them out with shades.
It makes the joy cry with shame
For other people's mistakes.
Why is the world so despicable?
It tears out the hearts of the innocent
And forces words into their heads.
It locks up so much happiness
And releases the beasts of despair.
It takes my favourite people
And makes their life so very unfair.
That's why the world is so cruel.

Sometimes you let your fear control you

- ***Sometimes you have to control your fear instead***

Time has always been something
That has crept into my brain
And scared me from the inside out.
And yet it is such a simple concept,
A measurement which exists in life
To keep track of where we have come from
And where we must go.

I think about time
More than it probably thinks of me.
When it is pushing me along,
Ripping my past from my hands
And forcing me to face the future.

I think about time in a way that is obsessive.
I think about each second as it ticks away.
I notice every minute of the day.
I check in every hour to check how long I have left
And each day ticks closer to an inevitable death.

But time is not my leader,
And I don't have to let it be in control.
I'm slowly (but surely) realising
That time can be put on hold.

Sometimes it is easy to focus on the bad things

- ***Sometimes you have to focus on the good***

I think its funny,
The way that humans behave.
How we complain about the weather.
How we take photos of the same sun,
Just as it sets in a different way.
How we like specific smells.
How we greet each other with a smile.
How we prefer specific colours.
How we have favourite humans.
How we all collectively agree on things,
And how we sometimes definitely do not.
How we really have no clue what to do
On this earth where we even question,
Why is the sky actually blue?
I think it's funny.

Sometimes you wish you could fix what is broken

- ***Sometimes you have to think about why it is broken***

I've always seen life as
Just a tragic novel for one,
With a weak plot and setting,
And the rest of the characters have gone.

Because I've had many chapters
Of the same broken book
And I'll just have to keep hoping
That the next chapter has some luck.

I may have little experience,
And my time may have been short,
But it's hard to feel optimistic when
Life is not playing out the way I thought.

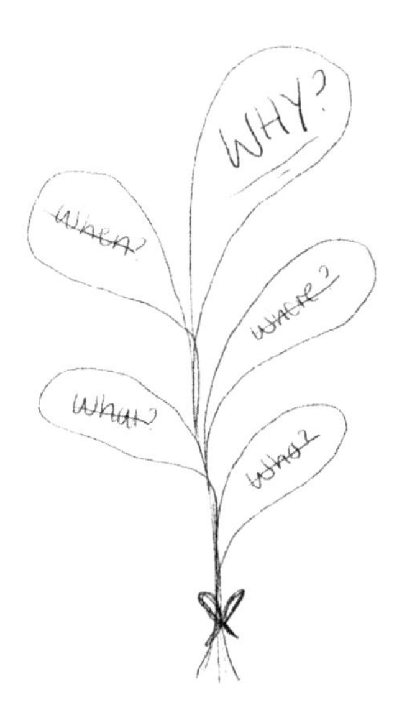

Sometimes you avoid the questions

- ***Sometimes you have to stop and wonder why***

When I was little they taught us
The five w's of questions:
Who, what, where, when and why.
And now that I am older I am
Learning them all over again.

Who am I?
What do I want to be?
Where do I want to go?
When do I want to get there?
And then I get stuck on why?

Because I guess I can say,
I am who I am,
I want to be a certain person,
I want to go to a certain place,
I want to be there at a certain point.
But I always get stuck on why?

Because why do I even want to try?
Why do I even care?
And why does everyone
Always ask why?

I Can't

Sometimes you are so sure you can't

- ***Sometimes you have to be sure you can***

I tend to tell myself
    I can't
Before I follow it with
    I can
And I assume it would balance it out.
But I've started to wonder if maybe
Starting with
    I can't
And then following with
    I can
Means that I believe
    I can't
And
    I can
Is simply a cover up.

Sometimes you doubt your experience

- ***Sometimes you think you have experienced too much***

I have not lived enough,
Seen enough,
Dreamt enough,
Breathed enough,
Existed enough,
To know the way life goes.

I am still young,
Still naive,
Still unaware,
Still confused,
Still hopeful,
To know everything life has to offer.

But in the time I have had,
In my short journey
And the trips I've made around the sun,
I have learnt enough for now,
To be at a stage where I take a moment
To be in reflection of life.

Sometimes you don't like to feel lonely

- ***Sometimes you just want to be alone***

I don’t like feeling lonely,
But I don't quite mind being alone.

I hate the emptiness
That is buried deep in my soul
And the dust that collects
Where my happiness should thrive.
That is the feeling of being lonely,
A deeper emotion
That is harder to resolve.

I love the peace
That settles around me
And the steady pace that I find
In the simple reliance I have on myself.
That is the premise of being alone,
Learning to exist
In your own quiet company.

Feeling lonely can break me,
But being alone sets me free.

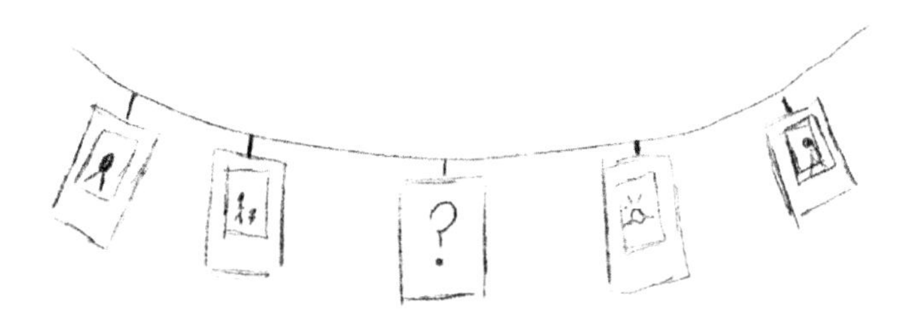

Sometimes you feel like you should know it all

- ***Sometimes it is okay to question things***

We act like we need permission
To question who we are,
To dare to be free,
To not know everything
We may set out to be.

We forget that it's okay
To wonder what will happen,
To leave some blank spaces
In the story we are still writing.

You're allowed to not know.
You're allowed to not want to know.
You're allowed to just be you,
If that's all you can bear to do.

Sometimes you say that everything is fine

- ***Not everything has to be fine***

We don't talk enough
About those days when
All you have to do is wake up
And you know the day is gone.
As the sleep weighs heavy
On the eyes that haven't opened,
And your soul feels empty
Of any hope or joy.

The days where life keeps moving,
But you aren't moving with it.
Where you watch your life
Like a bystander from the sidelines
And something tugs on your chest.

Nobody talks about how it feels
To feel nothing at all,
With no reason why,
And no way to help
Other than to let it pass by
And say that everything is fine.

Sometimes life is like a song on repeat

- ***Everyone has their favourite parts of a song***

I've always felt like
If my life were written out
In the form of a song,
It would start uptempo
With the freedom of childhood
And then it would get a little mellow
As the sorrow crept in,
With self doubt and insecurity,
And it would stay that way,
For a while at least,
Soft, simple and sweet.
Something you could dance to,
If you were really in the mood.
Something you could sob to,
If you felt like the world was against you.
A song with an end that loops around
And lets you repeat until
You feel like you understand the sound
And your soul has truly been found.

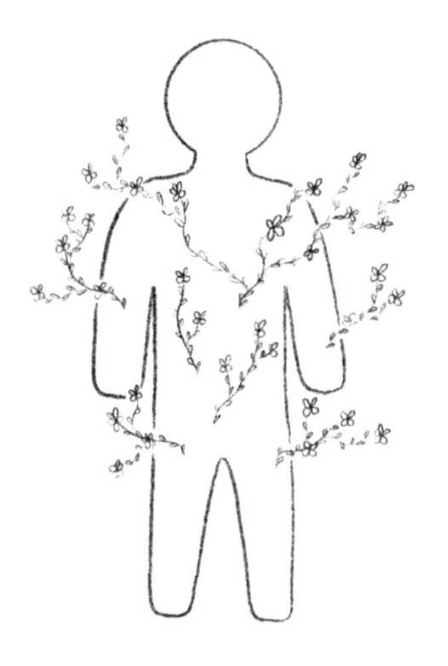

Sometimes it is nice to look pretty on the outside

- ***It is even better to be pretty on the inside***

I just want to feel pretty.
Not in the way that is
Plastered across billboards
Or highlighted online.
I want to feel ethereal.
Like I just stepped out of
A fairytale fantasy.
I want to feel like
My soul is glowing.
Not just that you think
I look good enough
For *you* today.
I want to feel beautiful
On the inside.
Like my insides have been
Carved out with sunshine
And my heart has been
Bathed in golden light.
I want to feel worthy
Of love and light and hope.
I want to feel pretty.

My heart's only competition

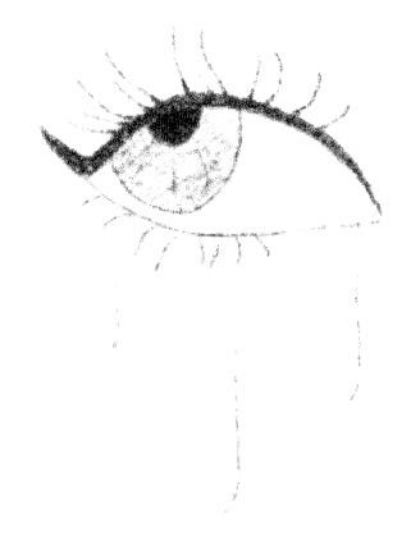

Sometimes it feels like your oxygen will end

- ***Sometimes you have to accept the reality***

It weighs heavy on my chest,
A thousand words,
A simple silence,
Pairs of eyes
And all the rest..

It weighs heavy on my chest,
A tugging at my heart,
A pull at my mind,
A competition with the beat
To finally be the best...

But the pace seems far too quick
And the words speed a mile
Trying to find the place to click
That fake mask into a smile.

But my breathing is rapid
And I don't know how to stop.
My thinking is erratic
And I can only think to panic.

Too many words,
Too much silence,
Too many eyes
And the world is losing its vibrance

….

Breathing **deep** and *slow*
But for how long?
My breath may flow
But in a short second,

It can all go wrong

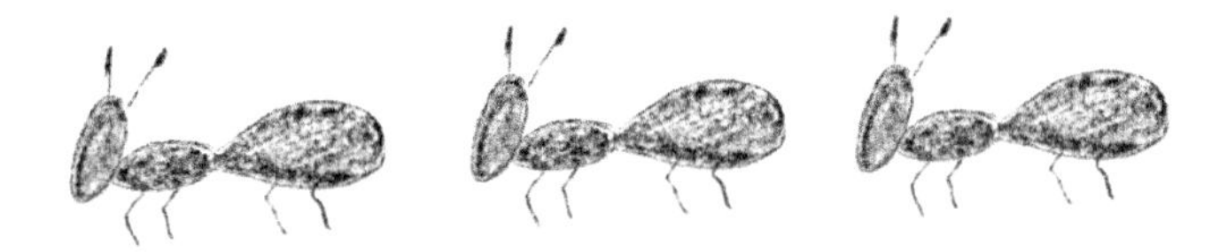

Sometimes you let the ants crawl all over you

- ***Sometimes you have to have the courage to brush them off***

It itches at my skin,
Crawls up my throat,
Sends shivers down my spine,

A feeling so prominent it could be physical
If it were not so caught up in my mind.

As if someone had grabbed me by the wrist,
Holding me back from moving forward,
Trapping me in this moment.

I am stuck in one position.
My mind racing ahead,
My body lost behind.

I should not be this affected
By the prospect of minutes ticking away.

And yet here I stay,
The same fear, another new day.

Sometimes crying is too much

- ***Sometimes the tears have to flow***

I've never been one to cry.
The rivers of emotions that flow
So effortlessly down the cheeks
Of so many people as a sign
Of their love, sorrow, joy and pain,
Run dry at the river bed for me.
I would love to say that I witnessed
Too much joy in the form of the sun
That it caused a drought of tears.
But instead it seems that I've had
Far too many storms than I can count,
That tears no longer accompany
The thunder and lightning of my thoughts.

But sometimes when I'm alone at night
And the darkness of the outside
Mirrors the darkness deep in my soul,
I feel the cool touch of one drop
As it slides down my cheek,
Singular and alone.

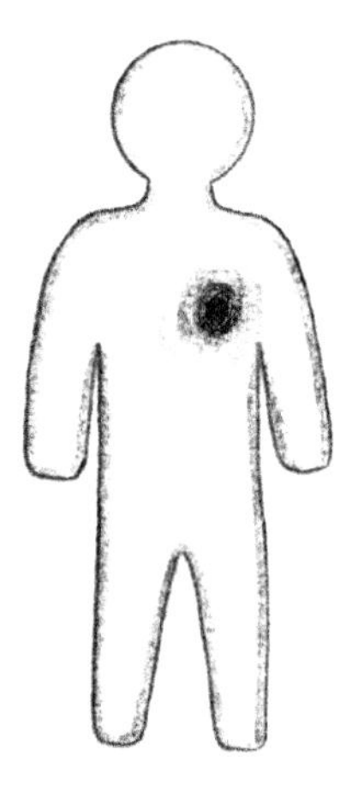

Sometimes you ignore the emptiness

- ***Sometimes you need to fill the hole***

There are days where I feel
So very empty on the inside,
Like I have been hollowed out
And left as a shell of my former self;
Fragile, delicate and easily broken.
And these days normally arrive
Without rhyme or reason,
And I spend all day
Interrogating my brain,
To find out why everything is gone.
Why the bliss of the last day
Has disappeared without a trace.
Why nothing is wrong
And yet somehow, everything is.

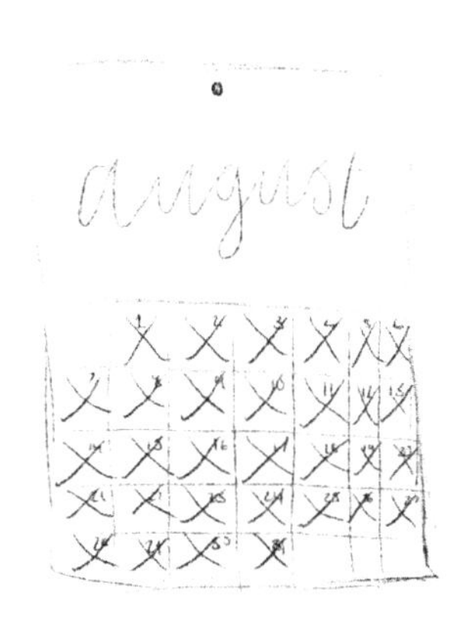

Sometimes you tick of future dates in your mental calendar

- ***Sometimes you have to look back at the memories***

As I get older,
I often let my thoughts wander
Beyond the present
And way into the future.
I forget my current worries
Just to focus on the ones yet to come.
Because as days pass
And they turn into weeks,
And weeks into months,
And months into years,
Time is not so slowly
Approaching all of my fears.
Even when I tear my thoughts away
From the spiral of my mind,
The future haunts me
Long after the thoughts have gone.

Sometimes you avoid what is obvious

- ***Sometimes you have to face it head on***

There is this voice inside my head,
Like an imaginary friend,
That tells me I won't succeed
And that all my dreams will end
In failure and misery.

The same friend is who causes the pain,
Stops me in my tracks,
Weighs me down, makes me feel insane
For trying to say a polite hello
Or catching a bus in the rain.

This friend is more like a stalker,
Following me around,
Whispering in my ear,
Making the silence seem so loud.

Anxiety is no friend,
It is my worst enemy.

Sometimes you detach yourself from the present

- ***Sometimes you have to live in the moment***

I have become a ghost of myself.
A sickly pale being floating around
As if I'm watching myself go along.
Listening from a mile away,
Existing from outside instead of within.
I seem to have lost my purpose
To the past of who I was
And the future that is already
Haunting me from ahead.

Sometimes a feather can turn your world upside down

- ***Sometimes it is exactly what you need***

Sometimes it is only subtle,
Like the touch of a feather
Brushing delicately on your palm.
A slight change in the atmosphere.
A difference in the pain,
Like a storm that is brewing in the distance,
Not fully prepared to destroy
But sitting so quietly in the background
That you notice its effort to be less aware.
This feeling that presses within me,
Telling me that something is really wrong,
Will not go away once it passes
And is something that is here to stay.
So I have to get used to that touch
That is as light as a feather,
And always bring an umbrella
Ready to brace the storm,
Just incase today is the day
That my nerves decide to erupt.

Sometimes you think about the terrible things that have been

- ***Sometimes you have to remember all the good that is to come***

Floating on a cloud.
But in a sense that feels literal,
Rather than the usual metaphorical.
In a way that feels neither,
Right nor wrong,
But just as though I have been evacuated,
Removed from my body,
And suspended in between,
My overthinking mind
And my sinking soul,
Its as though im resting
On a storm cloud.
Because at any moment,
My fragility and insecurity could
Strike in the form of lightning,
Or my sorrow and pain could
Drown me in its downpour.
But I guess at least it is a cloud,
A fluffy white one like the ones
Drawn next to the corner of a sun.
At least the worst has not been done.

Sometimes it is easy to pack your feelings away

- ***Sometimes you have to unpack what has been pushed away***

I tend to plan how to run away a lot,
Not in the way you may expect.

I don't plan to run away from home
To a place far away from here,
I plan to run away from my thoughts,
To stop them before they can get to me.
I plan to run away from my feelings,
Before they can take over my head.
I plan to leave it all behind.
In the hope that if I run away from them,
They won't be able to take control
And leave me vulnerable to
The strings that they attach
And the display that they create.

I plan to run away a lot.

Sometimes your emotions win the battle

- ***Sometimes your heart stays strong***

Not many things are able
To compete with the steadiness of my heart.
In fact one might say I'm a bit emotionless
And I'll admit it has some truthfulness to it.
Because I've never quite been able to connect
With the feeling buried in my soul,
But one thing that always manages to compete
With the steady hold of my heart
Is when it's forced to race against my mind,
In a quick paced competition,
To see what can cause me panic the quickest.
Will the thoughts that echo in my mind take over?
Or will the speed that my heart reaches,
And subsequently makes my lungs ache,
Panic me more when I can't feel myself breathing?
Which one will hurt me more?
Emotions can't knock me down,
But spiralling thoughts always will,
As they fight for the precious role of
My heart’s only competition.

Sometimes you think it is better to stay quiet

- ***Sometimes you have to let your words be free***

There are a lot of words,
That I keep in my mind,
That threaten to tumble
Right out of my mouth
And into the world,
If I only dared to push them.
But my apprehension overwhelms
My determination,
And my understanding that nobody
Else quite understands,
Is what stops me from
Letting go of all of my emotion.
Because I could say all
Of the things that I think,
But the likelihood that someone
Will get them, in the way I do,
Is so slim that I think
I'd rather just keep them,
Instead of speak them.

The people you meet along the way

The Good

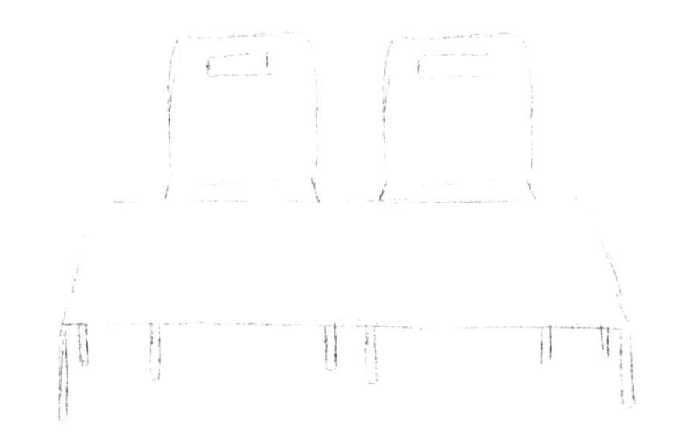

Sometimes you meet people that come and go

- ***Sometimes they go and come back again***

I met you when we were both naive,
In echoey halls and between classroom walls
When I struggled to breathe.

I learnt your name when you smiled at me
From across the room on a random day,
In a way that sets my soul free.

You became my friend when you let me in
And told me stories of present and past,
Filling me with comfort to the brim.

I really understood you after we fell apart
And then found our way back,

Beginning again from the start.

Sometimes you feel like you're holding the weight of thousands of raindrops

- ***Sometimes you meet someone who allows you to let it rain***

You are rain.
On a muggy day,
On a foggy day,
On that sickly sweet day in May.

You are rain.
Like thousands of teardrops,
Like floods of fortitude,
Like showers of sorrow.

You are rain.
When you wash away my worries,
When you drown out my thoughts,
When you promise for tomorrow.

You are rain, locked away with pain.
I am the clouds that let the rain remain.

Sometimes you get upset at wet footprints and storms

- ***Sometimes they don't matter at all***

I have always loved the way we
Balance each other out.
The way you know me
And I know you without a doubt.

When the rain pours,
I run from my place to yours,
Whilst you sit staring out from indoors,
As I track wet footprints onto the floors.

When my heart begins to race,
Just a bit faster than its usual pace,
And you greet me with your face
And my panic is gone without a trace.

When a storm gathers across your mind,
So I do everything in my power to find
Something to make you feel less confined
To the sorrow that is making you blind.

I love the way it will always be,
You and me,
A collective 'we',
Two people who set each other free.

Sometimes you feel more alone than ever
- ***Sometimes you're just one end of an unravelling ribbon***

The story of you & I
Goes a little something like this..

Two pairs of eyes,
Who had barely seen the world,
Found each other
In the crowded classroom
Of a brand new school.

Two minds that grew,
Both in sync,
To the ways and words
That were whispered in
The silence of summer.

Two hearts that connected,
As years went by,
Learning the beat and breath
Of how the other flowed,
Both in panic and in rest.

Two broken bodies,
Through emotion and sorrow,
Lost in a cavern of darkness,
Finding a way to the light.

Two smiles that shine bright
Enough to guide the other home
And find peace between the two people
Who started from the beginning,
To reach the end.

A hand that found the other
As they let go of the place they met
But did not leave the other.

Two souls that stay intertwined,
No matter the place, person or weather.

Sometimes home is a tangible thing

- ***Sometimes home is just a warm feeling***

There are some songs
That soothe your soul in an instant,
In the way that a hug might
Or a warm drink on a cold day.
Some songs are subtle,
In the way that softens my insides
And takes me away with them.
Some songs are pretty and delicate,
Like a light summer's breeze
Or a finger brushing hair behind an ear.
And all of these songs
Remind me of you.
A familiar tune,
A soothing soul,
A subtle touch,
And a delicate embrace.

Sometimes you let the sun shine

- ***Sometimes you have to shine in the sun's rays***

To be touched by sunlight
Feels almost like a dream.
Softening your soul with its essence,
Warming your soul with its glow.

But to be filled with sunshine
Is a blessing to all those around.
Beaming with the light you wish everyone could hold,
Enveloping people's hearts with your words.

Sometimes all that sunlight can be too much to bear
And clouds attempt to block your shine.
But as the rain falls,
And the sun escapes,
It makes sure that everything around it glows.

To be touched by sunlight
Is an honour to all.
To be filled with sunshine
Is a burden to bear.

But if raindrops and sun intertwine,
You may just find that rainbows fill the air.

Sometimes your heart is full of doubt
- ***Sometimes you find someone who sets it free***

I doubt the way that you feel for me,
Wondering if you feel the way I do
And then I see -

You read my favourite book
and tell me all the parts you adored,
You listen to my favourite song
And learn each and every word,
You know my favourite foods
And what I definitely don't like,
You text me every morning
And every single night,
You send me the moon
When we are miles apart,
You dance with me to our song
And then we do it all again from the start,
You send me sunsets
Because they make me feel in love,
You praise me and compliment me
Like I'm an angel sent from above.

And I finally know what people mean
When they say that they feel seen,
Because you see right through me
And you manage to set my heart free.

The Bad

Sometimes you want them to care

- ***Sometimes you have to accept that they never will***

I could tell you my favourite colour
And my favourite shoes
And my favourite way to do my hair.

I could tell you what I like to eat
And my favourite drink
And how I feel when summer fills the air.

I could tell you my middle name
And my favourite movie
And the perfect day if I had one spare.

I could tell you all these little things about me
And all the ways to make me smile
But it couldn't,
And wouldn't,
make you care.

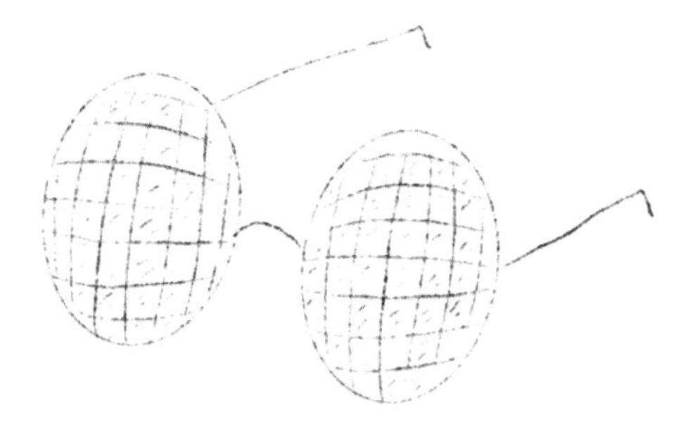

Sometimes you want to keep the glasses on

- ***Sometimes you have to see life without them***

In the past I have questioned
Whether the care that I receive is superficial;
A mask that is left on when I am around
And dropped as soon as I disappeared.
But I thought I had found safety in you.
I thought that for once it was mutual,
A bond that was held together
And safe from insecurity and hatred.
But I guess I was too quick
To paint a scene in golden light
And let my fantasy overtake reality.
Because as I drop my rose tinted glasses
I have begun to realise
That you are no different from my fears
And the trust I once held,
Was lost in the words you etched
Into the crevices of my back,
When you thought I wasn't looking.

Sometimes one text can break you down

- ***Sometimes one text can show you how to move on***

My eyes shine so much that
I can't read between the lines
Of your latest confession,
Of love or hate,
Or something in between.
My hands tremble
As if my whole world was shook,
And I thought you were my world,
So I guess the earthquake makes sense.
The worst part about it all
Is that you ended my world
In one simple text
That barely said what you meant.
But you know I overthink
And would read what you can't
Even bare to think enough
To say aloud to me.

Sometimes sorry speaks a thousand words

- ***Sometimes the sorries begin to stack up***

What good is sorry,
When you've said it once before?
What good is sorry,
When im laying on the floor,
Sobbing from being alone?
What good is sorry,
When you've made so many mistakes
That sorry doesn't mean anything anymore?
What good is sorry,
When it's done through a phone,
With no empathy or care?
What good is sorry,
When it doesn't seem fair?

What good is sorry
When sorry is the only word you know
And the only word I can't bear
To hear you say once more?

Sometimes you let your tears run down your face
- ***Sometimes you have to bottle them because other people are not worthy***

I have conditioned myself
To taste the salty tears
That brushed against my lips
The last time you let me down,
Every time we meet eyes.
Because you have a way of
Drawing me in with your look
And I cant be let down again,
Even if that means
That I have to relive
Every drop that fled my eyes
And every sob that escaped my mouth,
Just so the salty taste won't return.

Sometimes you look for validation in other people

- ***Sometimes you have to realise that it needs to come from yourself***

Your words warm my heart-
or at least they used to.

Every compliment and praise
Used to be like a hug to my soul.
Everytime our eyes would meet,
Or you would smile in my direction,
It would be like a blessing by the sun.

And now your cold glare,
And icy comments,
Freeze my heart instead.
I’ve cut out all the sunshine
And iced out the deeper emotion.

But I still seek the warmth,
For some reason,
And so I'll wait around *again*
Until you say something nice
And I can thaw my frozen heart.

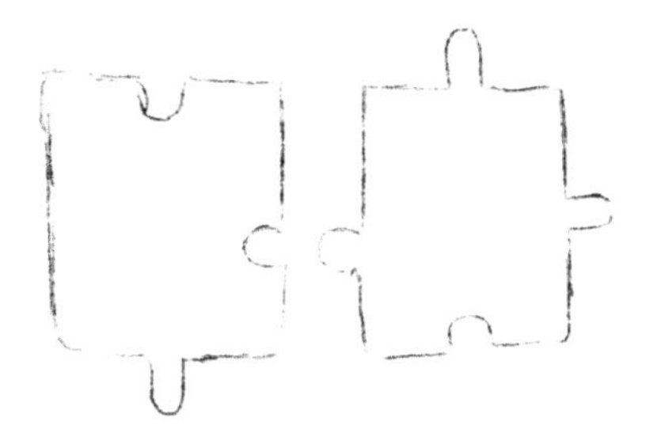

Sometimes you have to play along with their games

- ***Sometimes you have to bend the rule book***

I didn't mean to notice the patterns.
I didn't realise I was connecting dots.
But somehow when I did
I drew up a picture I think of a lot.
I just figured you don't talk that much,
I wondered if you might just be busy,
Everyone deserves space sometimes ,
But when does space become the whole galaxy?
You can tell me to stop.
You can let me know if I'm wasting my time.
I keep watching the time tick by
wondering if it's your problems or mine.
Am I reading too much into it?
Am I putting words where they're blank?
Am I adding you to my puzzle book
of the games I played when my heart sank?

Sometimes you try to knot your relationship back together

- ***Sometimes you have to let the rope fray***

It would be easier,
It would be simpler,
It would be quicker,
To break us off in one,
To take a straight cut,
To the ties between you & I.
But I can't and I won't.
Because I would rather
That it was harder,
That it was difficult,
That it was drawn out.
Because then maybe
It would mean more
Than you saying goodbye
On a random day in may.

Sometimes you worry too much about people who pretend to care

- ***Sometimes you have to fill out your own personality quiz***

You don't know me,
But you'll try to say you do.

You don’t know my middle name.
You don’t know my birthday.
You’ll pretend that your guess is basically the same.
You’ll ignore what I say.
You don’t know my favourite artist.
You don’t know the songs I repeat.
You’ll just guess the radio’s largest.
You'll just say the catchiest beat.
You don’t listen when I'm talking.
You don't understand why I care.
You'll just nod whilst walking .
You'll just shrug as though that's fair.
You don’t notice when I'm stressed.
You don’t notice when I disappear.
You just think that you know what's best,

And yet losing you is my biggest fear.

Leaving them behind

Sometimes you can let them have power over you

- ***Sometimes you have to recognise the power you hold***

I have never felt more alone
than between the hours of 12 and 3.
I have never felt more alone
than I do when your eyes gloss over me.
I have never felt more alone
than when I find it hard to breathe.
I have never felt more alone
than when I did when you decided to leave.

I have never felt more alone
and yet I am more often alone than not.

I always feel alone on those late nights
and yet I stay up as the hours pass.
I always feel alone as your eyes move
and yet I stare at you through the glass.
I always feel alone when I start to panic
and yet I let my oxygen drift away.
I always felt lonely when I was with you
and yet on that day I begged you to stay.

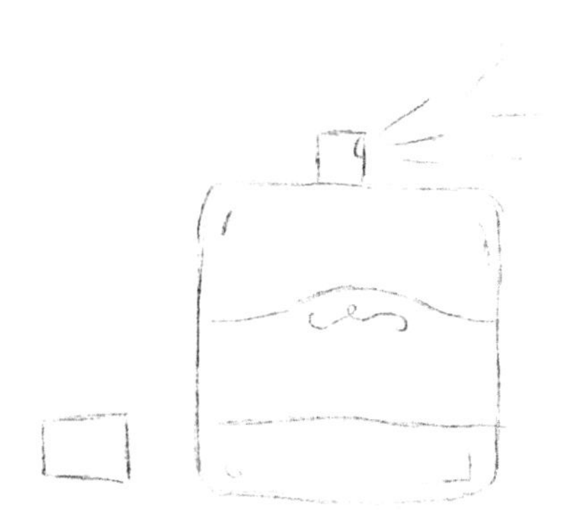

Sometimes you can be someones accessory

- ***Sometimes you can be your own person***

I hate the way you make me feel
~~Invisible~~
Like a line has been drawn through my name,
Like my soul has been erased.
Invisible
And yet somehow still right here,
But only existing as a waste.

A waste of what could have been,
A waste of who I used to be,
A waste of what everyone could see.

You make me feel
Invisible
The moment I step into a room.
But that makes me feel,
Invincible,
Because I no longer exist as an accessory,
Like a sweet smelling perfume.

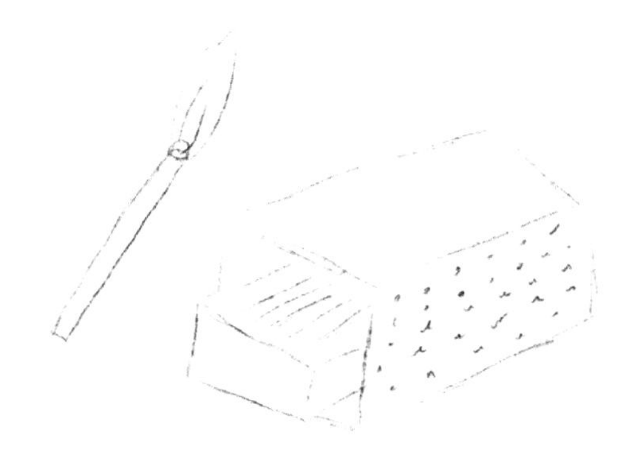

Sometimes you can fuel other people's fire

- ***Sometime you can let them burn out***

They say fight fire with fire
But I'd rather watch you burn
Because I lost all energy
To fight the battles that you light,
Back when your flame was just a spark.

They say fight fire with fire
But I'd rather drown you in water,
The salty sting of my tears
That accumulated each time
You lit a match once more.

They say fight fire with fire
But the passion within me
Burnt out so long ago
That all that's left for you to see
Is a pile of ashes
And to let fire die within me.

Sometimes you can smash the memories between you

- ***Sometimes you can frame them for the memory***

It's hard to hate you
When you were the one who
Taught me how to smile again,
To laugh again,
To breathe again.
It is so difficult to despise you
When you gave me the memories
I know will last a lifetime,
Beyond the existence of you & I.
I want nothing more
Than to wish the worst upon you,
But you showed me life's best.
And when you left,
You showed me life's worst.
So how could I dislike someone
Who still draws a smile across my lips
And allows me to really reminisce
On all the good and all the bad,
Of all the fun we ever had.

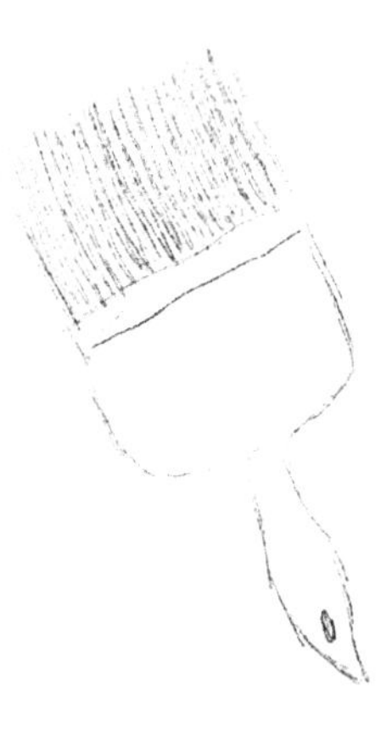

Sometimes you can let them paint a picture of you

- ***Sometimes you have to paint your own portrait***

You told me
That the best thing to do
Would be to set you free
And put distance between you and me.

But when I finally made that happen,
It was as if a switch went off in your mind
And suddenly you are the victim
And I am the suspect for this awful crime.

A crime that leaves you alone.
(But leaves me empty)
A crime where you are innocent.
(But I should have seen that coming eventually)

And now as you paint this picture,
I am still the one to blame.
But all I really wanted
Was for you to care for me the same.

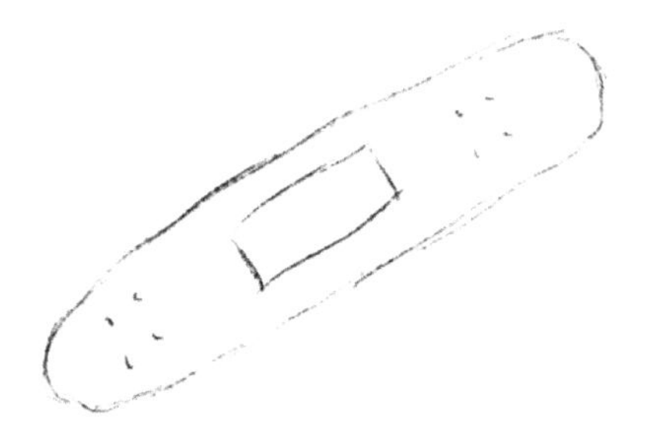

Sometimes you let them dig deeper into your soul

- ***Sometimes you stop them before they can***

When you left
It was as if the backstabbing
Had left an open wound.

A wound I struggle to cover up,
To heal or to mend.

Because for months
The knife has been stuck in the same place,
Causing me constant pain
But stopping the destruction of my body.

Now that you are gone,
So too is the knife
And the last hope I needed
To save this life.

I am broken down,
I am struggling
And now this open wound
Is a scar of who we are.

A constant memory
Of all the good

And a reminder
Of just how bad
The damage had gotten.

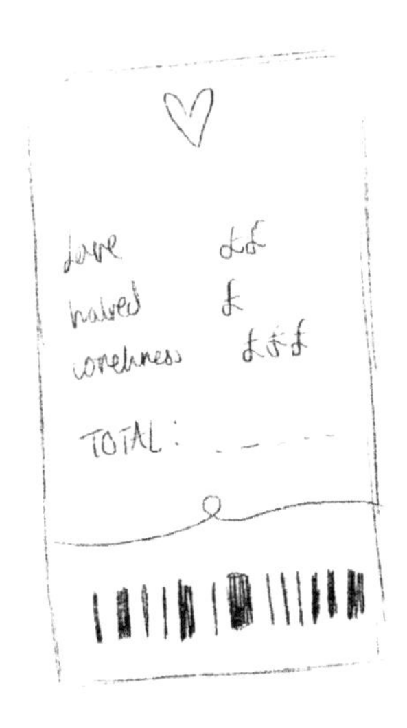

Sometimes you can wallow in what was forgotten

- ***Sometimes you have to force yourself to remember***

I could write three lists:
One for why I loved you,
One for why I hate you,
And one for why I miss you.

The first would be short,
The second a little longer,
And the last the longest of all.

Because I did love you,
And I still kind of hate you,
But not nearly as much as I miss you.

So I guess I don't really hate you,
And maybe I love you more than I thought.

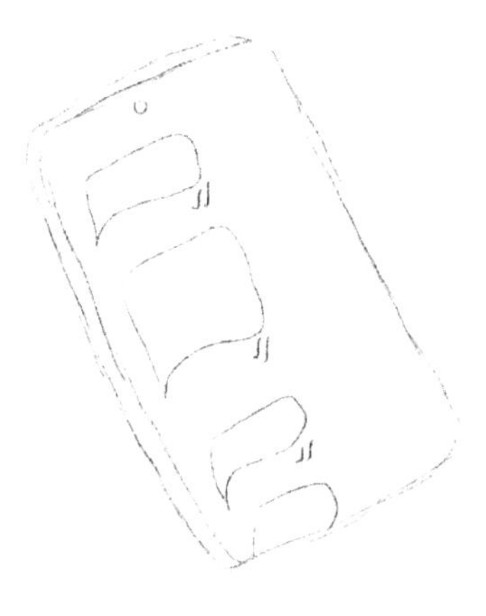

Sometimes you can give them all your time and energy

- ***Sometimes you have to leave them on read***

I have given one too many chances
To people who only give me glances
When I try to call their name.
And I have learnt that it is the same
When I am trying to hold their attention,
Because when I begin to mention
Anything revolving around me,
It is like they suddenly can't see
In my direction.
But they promise that isn't their intention
And they want to listen, they are sure.

But I don't think I want to talk anymore.

Sometimes you let people come and go

- ***Sometimes you have to close the doors into your life***

This time,
When you walk away,
I won't let you come back again.
So if you decide
That this time really is it,
Don't expect me to
Open my arms to you
And let you into my embrace.
Don't expect me to
Let you cry on my shoulder
And make me feel out of place.
When you walk away,
You walk away for life.

Sometimes goodbyes are hard

- ***Sometimes they're all we have left***

I can't even say goodbye,
Because the thought of you
Just makes me cry.
I have to be by your side.
So what do I do
When I want to hide?
Because you're not here anymore
And loving you
Was my only cure.
So in these words I will confide,
Now you are no longer
By my side.

I don't want to say goodbye.
All I keep asking is
Why you? Why?
And deep down inside,
I still have the overwhelming urge
To hide.
But once upon a time,
You told me that
Loving you was not a crime.
So now missing you
Will not be something I hide from.
It will be the only thing
I have left to do.

Sometimes you're set on things that should have happened
- ***Sometimes you have to let them go***

It's your birthday
But I don't know you like I once did.

I won't text you at midnight,
Recounting fond memories we shared.
No time will be spent
Pouring my heart into words handwritten in a card.

It's your birthday
And I always thought I'd be here for this one,
Watching you read the letter I wrote when I was sixteen,
Wondering how our friendship had evolved.

A year ago,
The connection between you and I
Was the be all and end all.

And now,
As the clock ticks slowly past midnight,
It marks another year alone.

Sometimes you can let them ruin every season

- ***Sometimes you have to reclaim what you love***

I've always loved what I call
The in-between seasons
Of spring and fall,
For many different reasons.
Because autumn is when
You broke my heart
And spring came around again
Giving me a chance to restart.

If you thought you could
Break me down
And I would
Let you see me frown,
Then clearly you forgot
The person I grew to be
The moment you let our love rot
And set me free.

So now as spring begins to arrive
And you try to reach out too,
I hope you see me thrive,
In another year without you.

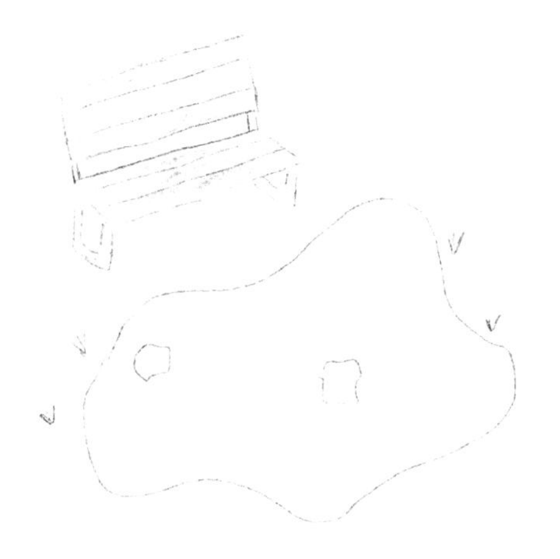

Sometimes it is hard to let a moment become a memory

- ***Sometimes a memory can be the way for a moment to last a lifetime***

The same echoey corridors
And the windows that creak,
The same laughter bounces off walls
And the cubicle I'd go to weep,
That one lonely bench to think,
I sit here now pondering,
Only enough to let my heart sink,
These are the things I'm left wondering.

The stuffy classrooms and halls,
The quiet hush of the staircase,
The air that travels when someone calls
And the secret code for just incase,
The gate to lead everyone away,
Letting us go out on the path we find,
And I'm not sure if I am okay
With growing up and leaving this behind.

Sometimes you can think that a heart once broken stays shattered

- ***Sometimes you can see that it can be fixed over time***

The day that my heart split
Into more pieces than
A glass that has been shattered
Against the kitchen floor,
I was so sure it could not be fixed.
I was ready to throw it all away
And let the shards tear away
At the little love I had left in me.
But somehow you came along,
With tape and glue and pins,
In the hopes of mending
My once broken heart.
And I'm not sure which method
Will actually fix it,
And I'm not sure how to feel.
Because you seem so ready
To help me pick up my pieces,
But I'm so scared
To put them back together again.

Dear…

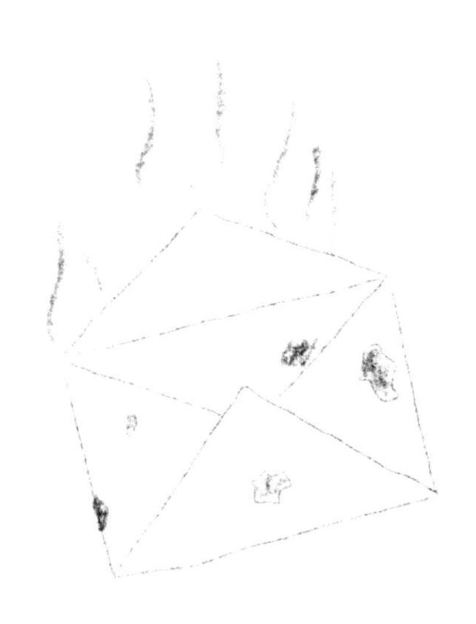

The person that I left behind

I would have loved to say
That our story ended
With you being here to stay,
With all our wounds mended.

I would have been the first one
To be by your side
On those days where you'd rather be gone
And the days you just wanted to hide.

I would have loved
To be the person cheering you on,
Showing you how you should
Be proud of how you shone.

But instead I stand alone,
Living life in the way
That you had thrown
Into the fire of that last day.

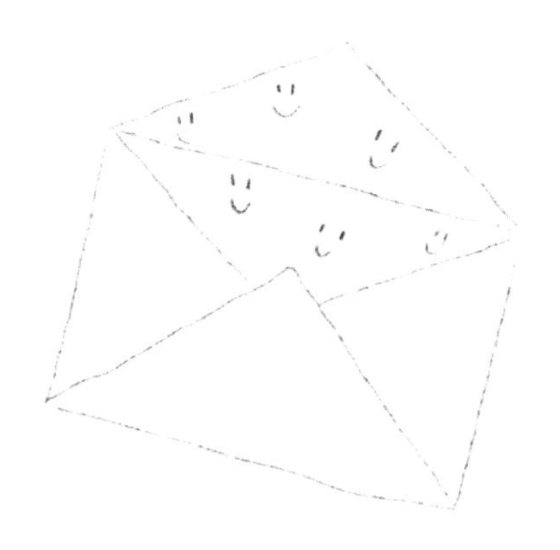

The person who left me behind

I should hate
The way you laugh with others
Whilst I'm left hollow,
The way you are surrounded by people
Whilst I am drowning in sorrow,
The way you've moved on
And I am left behind,
The way that you're in the future
And the past is stuck in my mind.

But even though I should hate
All the ways that you have changed,
I like to believe that fate
Has a special deal for me that has been arranged,
So that I can keep the memories of us
And move onto what is coming next,
So that I can let you move on plus
Keep the ghost of your smile and all the rest.

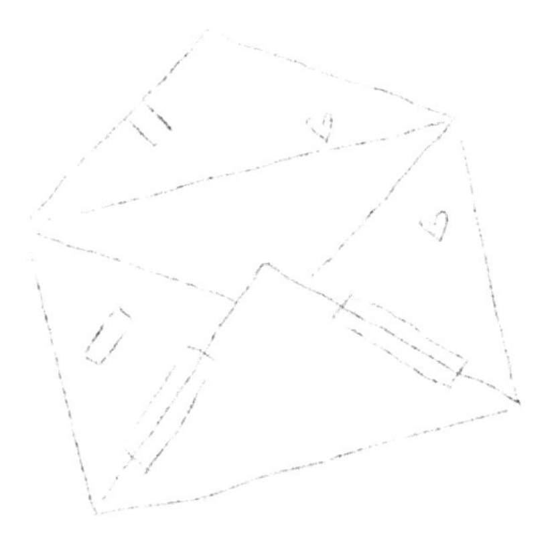

The person who I forgave whilst they forgave me

Sometimes we need the strength
To understand that this can happen.
Two people can make a mistake,
Both of them at the same time,
And work for forgiveness in sync.
Sometimes it's meant to be that way,
Like the world had decided it already
And made us break our ties,
To build back the ones we had already
Severed across the years, unaware.
I don't think that it's easy
To say that what's broken
Has been mended,
But I suppose you could say
That each wound
Has been stitched back together,
With a new thread that shines
Like opportunities, love and hope.
And in my eyes
That is almost better
Then fixing the things we broke.

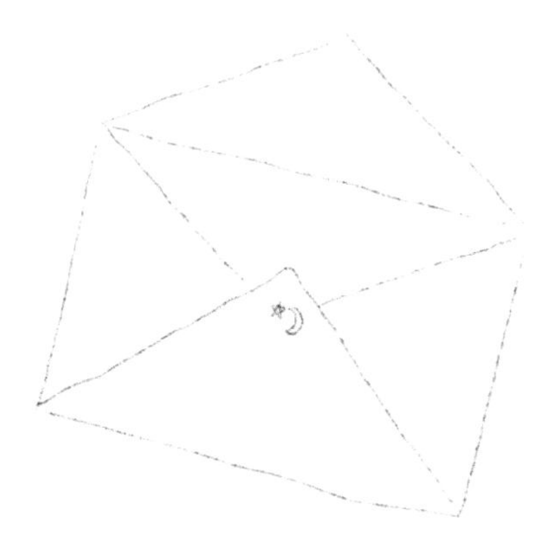

The person who I never thought I would meet

It isn't that I didn't want to,
It's just I never thought I'd get the chance.
And it's not like I'd never thought about it,
Because it is all that I have dreamed of.
But now you're less than a metre away
And my words have left my mind
And the comfortable silence
Is something I thought I'd never have.
And you were the person I had imagined
And the person I had grown to love
And the person I can now say is here for me
Both in person and in my head.

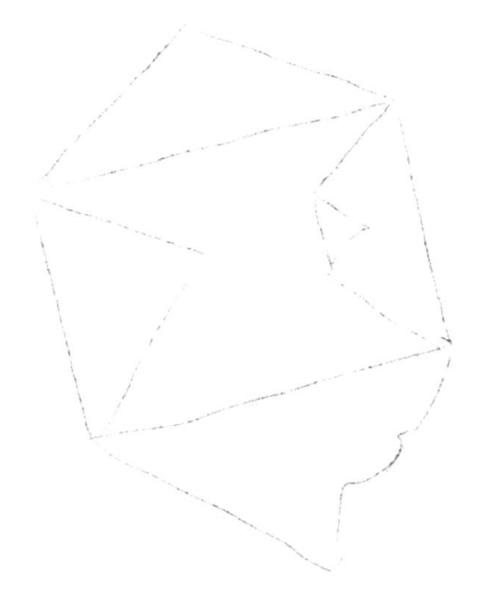

The person who hurt me

I have been knocked down before
And I always manage to rise again,
Like a fire rekindling from its ashes.
But when it came to you,
The embers became extinct in the fire
And I struggled to burn bright again.

It wasn't like I hadn't seen it coming.
Maybe I had been too naive to know
That you would send the words hurtling
The moment I came to my defence,
But at that moment I knew I had to go.

I was broken down and torn apart,
In a way that feels so physical,
And yet can only be metaphorical,
Something that burnt though my heart
And reminded me why we won't ever restart.

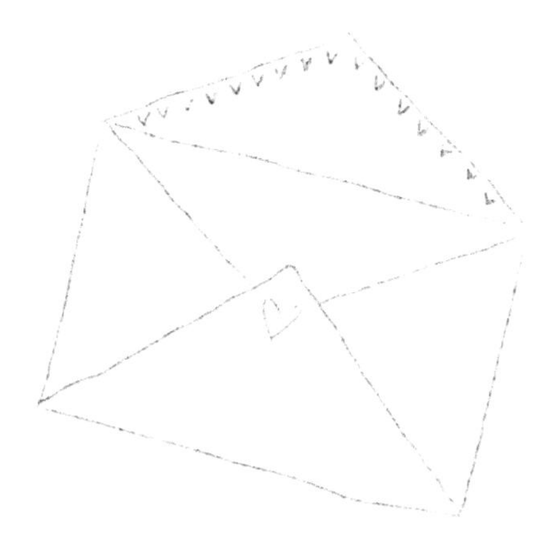

The person that means more than they know

Everyone has a comfort blanket
And I think you are mine.
The person I know I can always turn to,
Even if weeks, months or even years
Have gone between us.
I think I will always find a way
To stay in touch with you.
Because your words mean
More than you know,
And your smile means
More than you know,
And your laugh means
More than you know,
And your presence means
More than you know.

All I hope is that
Now you really know.

The person that I wish I could be

They say not to wish for change,
To look for something different
That isn't who you already are,
But in an ideal life
I think that is what I'd stand by.
I wish I could take it all in more,
Breathe a bit longer, in for more,
Take opportunities more,
Push the boundaries more,
Be the person who I want to be more.
The person that I wish I could be
Is the person that I can be,
If I draw out my potential
Just that little bit more.

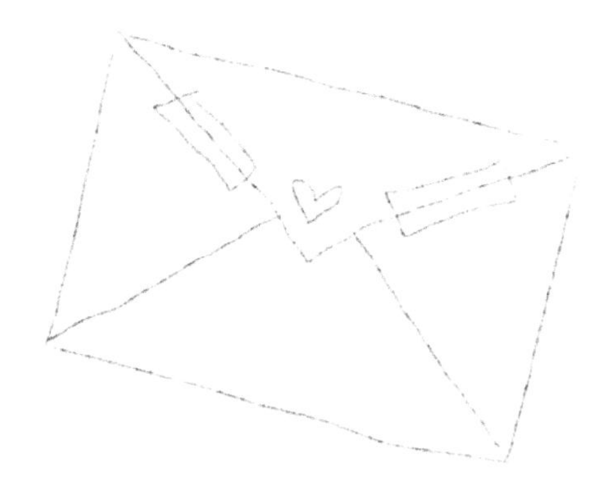

The person that I am proud of

It takes a lot of courage
To find your worth
And leave a situation
That is not built for you.
To build you up and give you love,
It takes a lot to see the wrong
And work to change it,
To find a place that gives you
Everything that you need,
To thrive after negativity.
And I am so proud
To watch you grow and bloom
Into a person who holds
So much joy and happiness
And to finally see you shine.

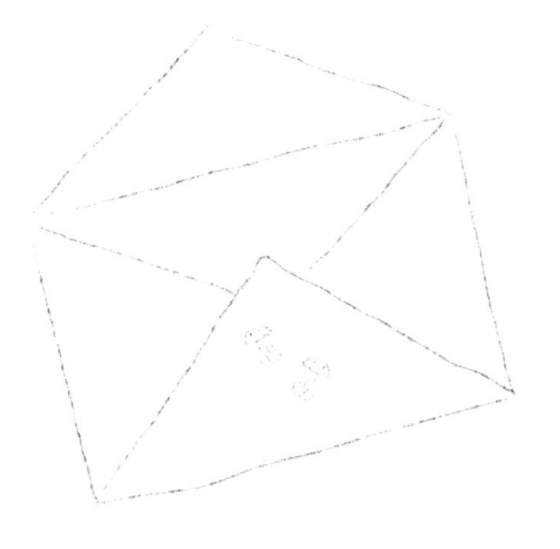

The person who listened

You barely knew me
And then I dumped out my feelings
And although it is wrong,
And I see that more now,
You still listened to it all,
Shared your feelings with me
And let me see what I couldn't before,
Whilst I showed you that you deserved more.
And still even 6 months on,
I owe you it all,
Because I am where I am now
Because you are there in case I fall.

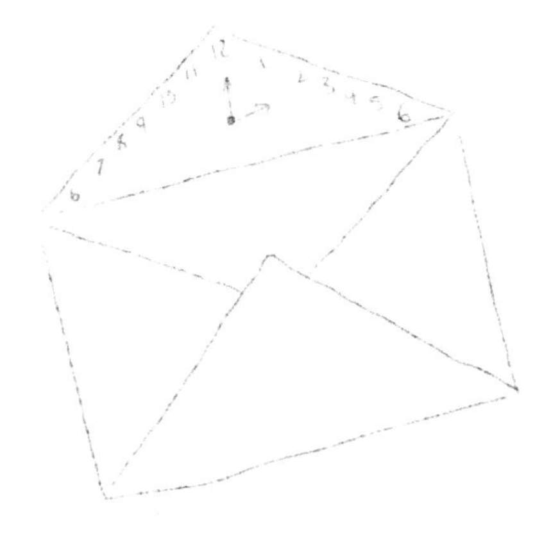

Time

I've always been in a one sided battle.
A battle between me and the abstract idea
That manages to control all of our hearts
And keep me so forcefully in the dark,
To the point where I spend hours of my life
Contemplating all the change that is yet to come
And all of the change that happened
Seemingly without me knowing.

I battle with these thoughts,
Every single day,
Whilst time carries on like nothing,
Like every second that ticks away
Is not leading me to my end.

I don't know why I fear you so much.
I don't know why you haunt me so often.
I don't know what frightens me every time
I glance up at a clock or calendar.
I do know that I want it to stop.

Give me back the time I have left.

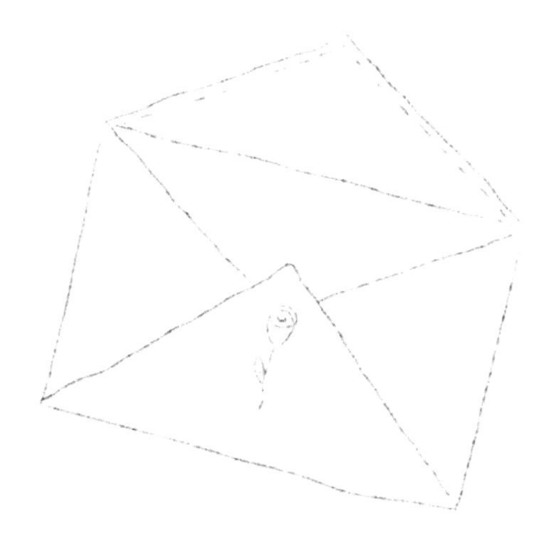

The people who made me who I am

There are a lot of things that go unsaid
Between the words of please, sorry and thank you.
There is a world of memories,
Special moments that only we will cherish.
There are laughs unlike any others
And smiles reserved for special occasions.
There are lessons that have been taught
And lessons always to learn.
No amount of words will ever speak aloud
The feelings that are buried deep in my heart
That convey every part of my appreciation
For the world that you made for me
And the person that you have allowed me to be.

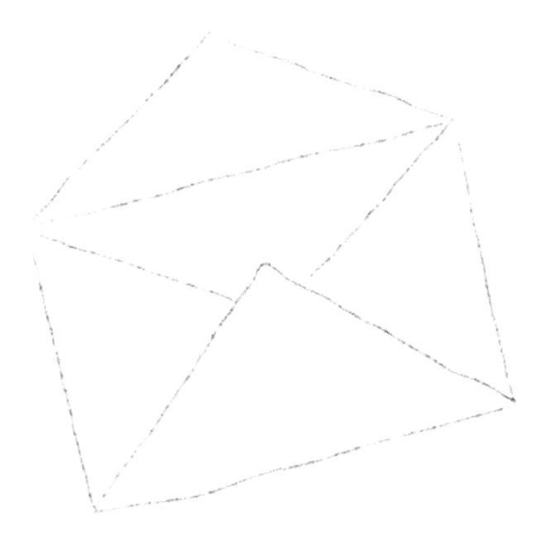

Myself

For years
You have spent your time
Focusing on how to make things better.
How to smile a lot more,
How to breathe a little clearer,
How to appreciate everything you get,
How to show other people that you care.
But I think that now is when
You start to realise
That everything you are already doing
Is already enough.
Nothing more is needed,
Just be the you inside.

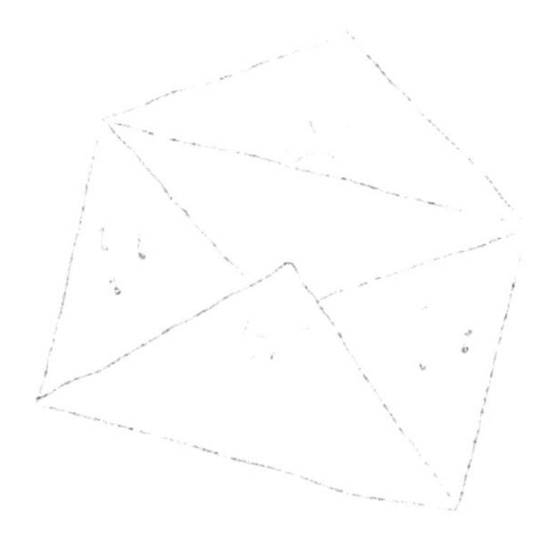

The person who was there through it all

When the sun sets or the sun rises,
It can turn any colour and it can be as dull
Or as vibrant as it wishes to be,
But no matter what it will always find the
Broken crack in my soul and thread a
New stitch of hope back through it again.

Ever since we watched the sun set together,
The feeling threads two stitches into the wound,
One for me and one for you,
Because the sun rising and setting
Means more now that you've seen it too.

A new book signifies new chances for new adventures.
The inky lines printed on fresh paper
Mould my imagination into scenarios
Of all kinds of wonder and enchantment.
No matter how close they brush to reality
Or how far they travel away,
The pages entwined in the spine of a novel
Have a second home in my heart.

Ever since my favourite books became ours,
The words connect to something more
Then the singular idea within my mind.
Finishing a book is more exciting
When you have someone to share the
Little details that made your heart flutter with.

The little things in life that allowed me
To keep pushing through my storms
Mean a whole lot more when I see them
not just through my eyes but also yours.

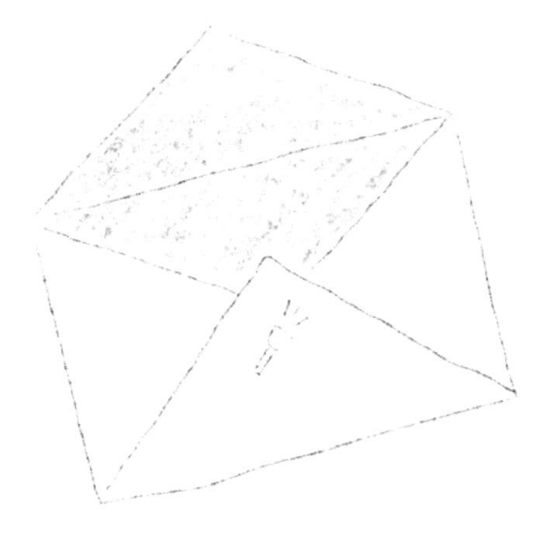

The darkness

Even though you have
Tried so very hard
To push me back into your grasp,
Time and time again,
I followed a different path,
Of growth and self-discovery,
To find out what I need,
To discover your weakness.

The weakness of light,
Of hope, joy and promise,
Of opportunity and acceptance,
Of finding who I am and was
And who I want to become.

Your weaknesses are my strengths.
And although I know that
We will meet again,
I also know exactly how
To escape once more.

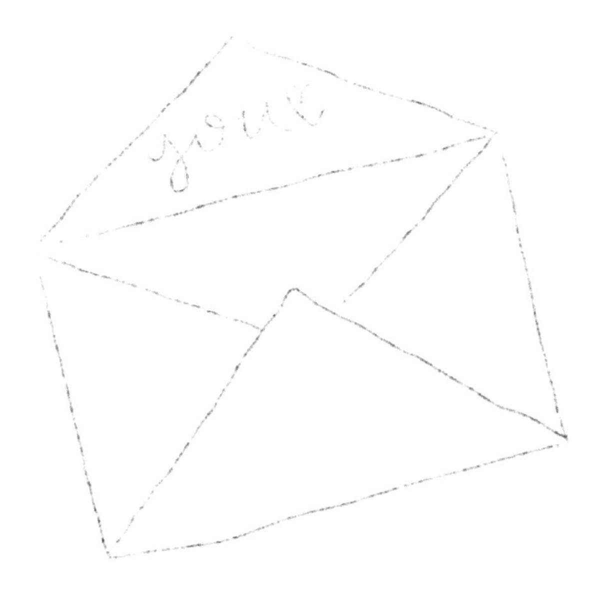
your

Dare to do what you believed you couldn't.
Look beyond the boundaries that you built.
Find a new way to rediscover
The you who you once buried within.

It is easy to climb into the darkness
Without closure and acceptance.
It is easy to accept defeat immediately
Without questioning what you need to fight.

Take a torch with you next time.
Light a candle when you're there,
Spark a flame within you
And don't let the darkness rip you apart.

When the world goes dark
I try to imagine all the happy things
Which cause me to be here today.

When I doubt the love that I receive,
I think of my 9th birthday,
When everyone gathered around to create something special
For me.

When I doubt the friendships I have made,
I remember the laughs and smiles
That populate the faces of those around
When I am there.

When I doubt my successes,
I remember that I have made it through
18 whole years
Of breathing, eating, sleeping and living
To be here.

So when the world goes dark,
I find the things I need
To turn the light on.

This was a letter,

To all the tears that I had cried and the words I found comfort in,
To the lunchtimes I sat alone and poured out my emotions,
To the times I stared at a bright screen before me,
(this book is all of that and all of me)
To forgotten friendships and found families
To book pages and book friends,
To the moon in the sky and the one miles away from me,
And to my family who made me who I am.

Acknowledgements

This book is a collection of my thoughts and experiences in the last year of my life. I am still young, with so much left to learn and discover, but this year in particular has been one that I had to push to overcome. Poetry has been my lifeline throughout the struggles that I had to face, and this is the journey that I went on.

Thank you for reading my words and hopefully they mean as much to you as they do to me. No matter how I intended them to be read or understood, you have the power to shape those meanings into something you have experienced. Take a hold of your darkness and let the light take it away.

Special thanks go to my friends and family for their continued support of my writing and words. I would be unable to achieve what I have without their encouragement to continue.

Thank you to Emily for your constant support and for being there when poetry was not necessarily enough.
Thank you to Katie for being a constant inspiration for my work and for being there despite the challenges we may face.
Thank you to Alishba & Anisha, for being people I can talk to when the world gets dark.

Thank you to Sacha, Vi and Iris for your constant support from miles away.

And lastly, thank you to my mom, dad and sister for always being the ones to believe in me no matter how big my dreams may be.

About the author

Emily Weaver is an 18-year-old aspiring author and poet. She has always held a strong love for writing and reading and developed a passion for poetry in the beginning of 2021.

She shares her poetry online on social media. Ranging from poems about love and growth to loss and despair.

'Leave the light on' is her debut poetry collection written across 2022 and 2023. It follows her reflection on her experience
of the past year and shares this journey with the reader.

Aside from poetry, she is working towards finishing her debut novel as well as fueling her reading habit. She enjoys listening to music and watching the sunset.

You can find her on social media:
@canvasofthesky